Free Verse: A Poetic Vision

Latoni Hatch

BookLeaf Publishing
India | USA | UK

Presentation by *BookLeaf Publishing*

Web: www.bookleafpub.com

E-mail: info@bookleafpub.com

ISBN: 9789357444996

First edition 2022

Poetic Soul

Peacefully writing
is peacefully dying.
Otherwise,
it is forever frightening.
I realize,
we are all expiring.

Keeping an elevated mind
with thoughts aspiring
to beat
the world's clock and movements.
They are tiring.

Within political agendas
created for dividing,
you find an intelligent poetess
with lyrics devising
a plan
to revamp a spirit colliding
with chaos
and violence.

A poetic soul is inspired by surviving.

Birth of a Poem

This feels like freedom
though it came from entrapment.
You like how it sounds
I like it as combatant.

My poetic soul
full of triumph and passion
though physically set in a world of distraction,
goes sifting through words to achieve extraction
Not realizing til it's over exactly what happened.

Advice

Life sings and yells
Bringing bliss and bringing hell
Live
and balance well.

Travels in June

Is it ok for me to go on a journey?
Is it ok for me to cruise?
If I spread my eyes across the ocean,
will it get rid of all my blues?

Is it bad to sail for clarity,
and still come back confused?
In my bottle of ocean sand,
is there any time to lose?

The silence of ocean waves,
are they supposed to make that sound?
And if I float in the water
do you promise I'll never drown?
What about just my toes?
may I dip my foot in?
Do you mind if I just sit back?
Smile, and pretend?

This is not to my comfort,
I don't like this at all.
They said life's a beach.
Well, I'm just salty is all.

Plenty sea shells in my bucket,

but few treasures to awe.
How selfish of a thought,
I do everything wrong.

Gasp

When you think this deep,
there is no coming up for air.
And even though you surface,
you still don't feel there.

Heavy Weight

There was a tragedy in me,
one I wouldn't want you to see.
Simply because,
it's embarrassing.

But the more that I seek,
the more clear it becomes.
That neither one of us
is slightly above.

All things, which plague the human condition.
The mind, body, soul,
things like addiction,
bsession and ignorance.
all of life's lessons,
but also the miracles,
commonly called God's blessings.

No one else,
all are missing
when it's your turn to fight the battle.
Not the one against the world,
But the one within that matters.

Every man or woman for self.

Each hasn't really anyone else.
No other
to do the things that must.

This is the daily spinning,
The round and around.
A round for round
Fight
For
Your
Life.

Day Dreamer

Is it just me or are day jobs the worst?
How come nobody taught us
that our dreams come first?

Chase After Freedom

Dreams keep me distracted
Never suck up to a boss
Quickly, I quit.
No submission,
as they thought.

Don't I get to choose?
"Just do what you've got to".
But who says I gotta?
A difference between me and you.

Mentality is everything.
They say to me, mentally ill.
Walking in the worst way.
Hearing my confidence with
a resounding shrill.

Me, I refuse,
though consequences do weigh.
These times and rhymes,
are all covered in gray.

If I can't chase what I'm after
I'm dead anyway.

Desire For Change

Wanna be free
in me again.
Free in my mind
before the world told me it's truth,
sugarcoated in lies.

Not enough room for all the tears in my eyes.
I've seen too much.
Filled with regrets
over the things I've touched.

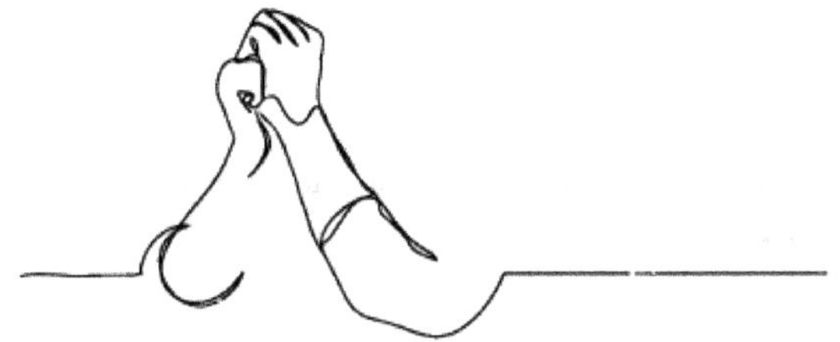

In The Eyes of Depression

What do they really know about depression?
A google search?,
An ad on television?

Or maybe a meme,
that could seem funny to me.
and then remembering
a true living hell.

Oh well.
You see,
they never could tell.
They required notice instead.
Never truly knowing
this nature inside their head.

You/Me/I

You have seen your reflections of ugly and
bitter.
You let them fade to dust and you watched them
turn to glitter.
You dispersed them from your hands, cleansed
yourself of that material
You walked away, and to your burdens gave no
memorial.
You found purpose in your toil.
You found growth as with harvesting from soil.
You cried nights of terror.
You reexamined errors.
You eliminated certain traits.
You kept moving in dire straits.
You have absolutely all it takes.
You move as if there is no wait/weight.

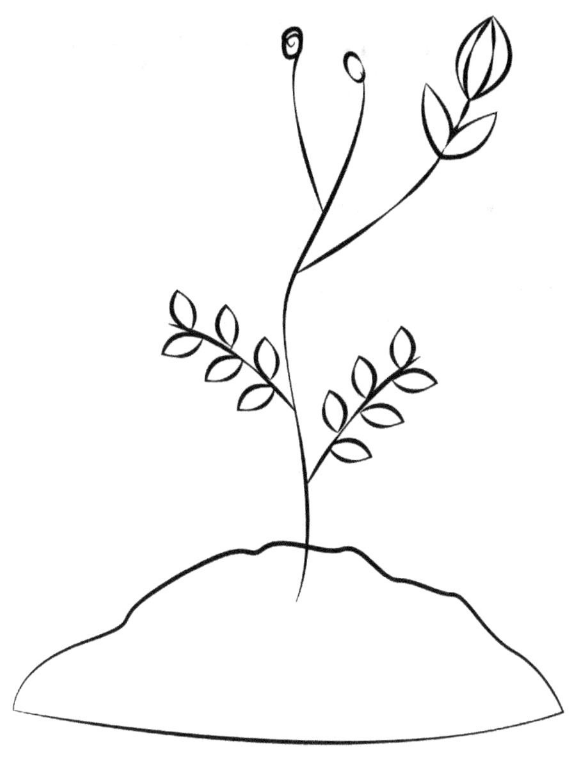

A Heart For Love

Don't know what I will do.
He's haunting my dreams.
In the best kind of way.
I like seeing his face.

Told myself I wouldn't do it.
Said I wouldn't pursue.
But here I am being silly.
Writing poems for you.

A Haiku

Without excitement.
One might say I am quite bored.
Procrastination.

Haiku: Creation

Sitting in my room,
words are written on notepads.
Silent creations.

Haiku of Love

Long lost heart of mine.
Is it you or I that hides?
As if love is crime.

Haiku: Heartache

I am all alone.
My heart and mind are in shock.
Impossible love.

Haiku For Son

You are my child, son.
You hold my heart and my pride.
I dream you are great.

Haiku For My Daughter

You are my daughter.
With you, I fight my old self.
I have confidence.

www.ingramcontent.com/pod-product-compliance
Lightning Source LLC
La Vergne TN
LVHW051250200726
843510LV00011B/1773